CHRONOLOGY OF RECENT HEALTH CARE LEGISLATION

HOW NOT TO REFORM HEALTH CARE

Fran Haddy

authorHOUSE®

AuthorHouse™
1663 Liberty Drive
Bloomington, IN 47403
www.authorhouse.com
Phone: 1-800-839-8640

First published by AuthorHouse 6/24/2010

ISBN: 978-1-4520-3545-1 (e)
ISBN: 978-1-4520-3546-8 (sc)

Library of Congress Control Number: 2010908634

Printed in the United States of America
Bloomington, Indiana

This book is printed on acid-free paper.

TABLE OF CONTENTS

The Players

Health reform had a rocky start in the White House. President Barack Obama nominated South Dakota Senator Tom Daschle as Secretary for Health and Human Services (HHS) because of his extensive experience in health and in Washington, DC. Shortly thereafter Senator Daschle withdrew his nomination. President Obama then nominated Kansas Governor Kathleen Sebelius for the position. She was confirmed by the Senate only after some delay. In the meantime President Obama created a new office in the White House, the Office of Health Reform. He named Nancy Ann DeParle, M. D., director of that office (not requiring Senate confirmation; it's said that she had been working on health reform for a month prior to creation of the office). He also named American Medical Association (AMA) member Howard Koh, M. D., Assistant Secretary of Health in the Department of HHS.

OBJECTIVES

The AMA leadership met with DeParle and advocated six key health reform objectives: health insurance coverage for all, quality improvement, reformed government programs, reduced costs, promotion of wellness and prevention, and delivery system reforms. DeParle reinforced the administration's commitment to work with the AMA and the physician community to adopt policies that would foster quality and affordable coverage for all. The administration would continue to press for Medicare physician payment policy changes to end the annual battle to avert steep cuts and DeParle stressed that action on many key physicians' policy objectives would be determined by the outcome of the broader health reform debate. These views were formalized and expanded in a letter to President Obama on April 13, 2009. There were now eight (instead of six) views: protecting families' financial health, making health coverage affordable, aiming for universality, providing portable coverage, guaranteeing choice, investing in prevention and wellness, improving patient safety and quality, and maintaining long term fiscal sustainability. The AMA highlighted three areas: liability and costs, building on the current employer-based system, and examination of antitrust barriers and quality.

DEMOCRATIC DIVISION

Some of these health issues were seen as possibly dividing the Democrats when Congress reconvened after a two week break. For example, Democratic leaders agreed that they were further along on a wide ranging overhaul of healthcare than they were on Obamas' revolutionary climate change agenda. Senator Max Baucus (D-MT), chair of the Senate Finance Committee, had been holding talks on health with insurance, labor, hospitals, and—perhaps most important to key Republicans—lawmakers. "But Senator Charles E. Grassley (R-IA) warned that proposals for a governmental-funded competitor to private insurers and a healthcare board with broad powers could meet GOP resistance. In addition, Democrats were sure to incite Republicans if they adopt the budget in the reconciliation process, fueling charges that "Obama has ditched bipartisanship."

Some experts preferred free-market alternatives to universal healthcare, saying every provider group with a lobbyist, from massage therapists to fertility specialists, would want in. The result would be expensive insurance policies and costly government subsidies.

The House and Senate did in fact pass congressional budget resolutions. The House version contained provisions that would facilitate the passage of legislation to replace the flawed Medicare physician payment formula, known as the sustainable growth rate (SGR). The AMA strongly advocated for the inclusion of these provisions.

The AMA also supported a plan of action for promoting health care quality. On April 1, 2009, the AMA and other state and medical specialty organizational boards sent a plan of action to President Barack Obama and congressional committees involved in health care issues regarding steps the medical professions will take in the coming months to engage and support physicians in quality improvement methods. These steps included a commitment to education and other activities.

Regional health reform forums continued. The White House's fourth regional forum on health care, held in Greensboro, NC, focused on health care costs. The forum was moderated by DeParle and Governor Bev Purdue. DeParle said it must be bipartisan and supported by all stakeholders. The fifth and last forum was held in Los Angeles. The previous ones were in Michigan, Vermont, and Iowa.

Public Insurance Plan

Senate Finance Committee Chair (D-MT) Max Baucus' most controversial proposal—which was supported by the other committee chairs—called for the creation of a public insurance plan that would compete against private insurers. This contentious issue divided Democrats, who wished to enlarge the government's role in health care, from Republicans, who favored more market-based solutions. Most Republicans on the Senate Finance Committee, including its ranking member Senator Charles Grassley of Iowa, senior Senator Orrin Hatch of Utah, and Senator Michael Enzi of Wyoming, also serving on Senator Kennedy's health panel, were strongly opposed. Grassley said that the creation of a public plan was a "deal breaker" for Republicans if it's in and a "deal breaker" for the Democrats if it's not. Is there a compromise in between? "I don't see one today."

EXPERT OPINION

Charles Krauthammer said Obama's health care plans will require rationing. "Taken as a whole, Obama's social democratic agenda is breathtaking. However, to pay for nationalized healthcare and federalized education, what is absolutely required is entitlement reform." Making cuts in social security is relatively easy. "However, Medicare and Medicaid cuts will require rationing."

Dr. Thomas E. Starzl, one of the fathers of organ transplantation, said the foremost problem of health care is cost, and Dr. Mark Siegle said lack of acceptance of Medicare illustrates the weakness of universal health care. Congressional leaders issued a letter objecting to Medicare payment shifting from specialists to primary care physicians. California awaited federal help in health reforms. Governor Schwarzenegger and the legislature abandoned any serious attempt at health reform.

Cost Reduction

Some researchers believed that health care costs could be reduced by a stunning 30 percent or about $700 billion a year—without harming quality if we moved as a nation toward the proven and successful practices adopted by the lower-cost geographic areas and hospitals. The Mayo Clinic was cited as one of the medical centers providing care for chronic diseases at low cost.

CREATING VALUE

The National Symposium on Medical and Health Reform met in Rochester, Minnesota on April 27, 2009, and concluded that creating value for the patient, co-ordinating payment reform, and insurance for all were important matters to health care. The *Washington Post* (April 27, 2009) editorialized, "Of the many possible issues that could defeat healthcare reform, one of the biggest is whether the measures should include a gov-ernment-run plan."

The Mayo Clinic Health Policy Center concluded early in February that we should stop paying for indi-vidual procedures and instead pay for whole (better) outcomes, safety, and service at lower cost.

DEMOCRATS DISAGREE

It appeared that infighting among Democrats was impeding healthcare reform. The disagreements surrounded "whether to create a new government-sponsored insurance program to compete with present companies." Recently more than 70 House Democrats warned party leaders that they will not support a broad health reform bill that does not offer consumers a government-sponsored policy, and two unions withdrew from a high profile health coalition because it would not endorse a public plan.

Senators Baucus and Kennedy said healthcare overhaul will be written by June, 2009! A columnist in the *Wall Street Journal* said the chances for healthcare reform by year's end are "surprisingly good." The question of government-sponsored insurance dampened this optimism.

Physician Supply

The *New York Times* considered how medical school students are preparing for health reform challenges. Admissions will rise but the recruitment pool is limited, partly because fewer students are applying for available medical school positions, and there are financial constraints at the level of the hospital residency programs. It seems possible that youngsters are no longer attracted to medicine as a career, which would among other things, lead to a decrease in quality. Patients and some physicians are more attracted to alternative forms of medicine, and an accurate accounting of the costs of this type of medicine is difficult to generate. Sums as large as $34 billion per year (2007) were mentioned, without the current rate of increase. The current rate could be considerably larger.

DEMOCRATS PLAN

Congressional Democrats released health care reform plans, and Senator Baucus said plans will likely contain taxes on some employer-provided health benefits. Peter Orzag of the Congressional Budget Office (CBO) said healthcare spending will be deficit neutral over the years. Polls showed strong support for federal health care, but the AMA was wary of public health insurance. A surtax on the rich also emerged as a health care option.

"Senate Finance Committee reached 'broad agreement' on how to slow rising health costs." They constructed a detailed set of recommendations "that are intended to force changes to slow the growth of Medicare and hold doctors and hospitals accountable." The budget plan supported use of "reconciliation" for health reforms. This would allow Obama's proposed health care overhaul to move through Congress immune from filibuster. In spite of "broad agreement," Republicans objected to this fast track reconciliation process on a matter as sweeping as health care, but Democrats said they will use it only if bipartisan negotiations break down. They have until October 15 to produce their reconciliation bills. But the Senate Committee plans to produce their stand alone bill in June.

George Will said that reconciliation for major health care reform is a misuse of authority and the Democrats use of the reconciliation process for major reforms is a misuse of authority.

Some Republicans were seen as cooling to health reform, i. e., the inclusion of reconciliation closes the door on good bipartisan health reform.

Medicare Funds and Other Matters

Finance Committee Chairman Max Baucus (D-MT) questioned the Center for Medicare and Medicaid Services' (CMMS) capacity to design Medicare overhaul and suggested a "new entity" in charge of designing major changes in the Medicare system as part of the health care overhaul. The financial outlook for Medicare was seen as raising "serious concern" and Medicare's trustees may soon warn Congress that they may run out of money by 2019.

Teamwork and interdisciplinary training were emphasized at the Mayo Clinic national symposium on medical and health care education reform. Everything from education to care delivery should be built around the needs of the patient.

The *New England Journal of Medicine* published three perspectives on comparative effectiveness research (CER). The proposal to include $1.1 billion for CER in the federal stimulus package resulted in vigorous debate, requiring more understanding of this ill-defined area.

Cost

Cost was seen as the primary obstacle to health care reform. The up front tab could reach $1.2 trillion to $1.5 trillion over 10 years, while expected savings could be slow to appear. Republicans were seen as still considering conservative alternatives to the public insurance option and searching for rhetoric to attack health care reform. Obama's budget proposal includes $879 billion for HHS. The proposal called for increased spending to fight Medicare fraud.

There was a lesson from Massachusetts. After two years, the state's health care reform got mixed reviews. At stake ultimately is whether the Massachusetts reform can survive if health care costs continue to rise. Costs continued to increase; control was not tried.

The health care industry pledged to reduce the increase in costs. The pledge was to save $2 trillion over ten years. The industries included the AMA, the AHA, health insurance companies, device manufacturers, and others. The aim in part was an attempt to get a seat at the bargaining table.

Fiscal Suicide?

David Brooks said President Obama was actively spending, hoping for savings from health care later on. Savings from health care are speculative, distant, and uncertain. Without serious health care cuts, this burst of activism will hasten fiscal suicide.

Krauthammer said essentially the same, based on CBO data. The cries for postponement increased. President Obama said, "Don't count us out just yet." However, when congressmen encountered constituents on home territory during the August break, it became apparent that there were still many questions to be answered concerning the health plan, in particular, funding and the proposed public health insurance. It appeared prudent to some to postpone and/or reduce the scope.

Physician Shortage

There were other important areas still to be explored. According to family doctors, patients trying to save money are getting sicker before they seek care. Some say the problem of primary care physician shortage should be first addressed. Is it related to the decrease in medical student applications? It's said that there are now only two applicants for every position, where at one time there were ten to twelve per position. Are students no longer interested in medicine? Are we no longer getting the most and best applicants?

Are we gradually replacing our highly trained MD physician pool with less well trained non-physician practitioners? How much does alternative medicine cost? In 2007 it was $34 billion.

Advertising

Should advertising for prescription drugs on television and on the internet be banned? It's said that the number of prescriptions for unnecessary and inappropriate drugs has increased since regulations were loosened in 1997.

Senator Kennedy

Terminally ill Senator Edward Kennedy sought a quicker replacement. Daschle returned to a spotlight in health debate. The former senator from South Dakota emerged as a key player at the White House and Capital Hill, sparking questions about possible conflicts of interest.

Debate at
the Local Level

Debate continued at the local level during the congressional recess. The "public option" polarized the debate. "Public option" could be government insurance to balance private insurance and "co-ops" in theory would be owned and operated by millions of policyholders. The debate at the local level was surprisingly vigorous and could not help getting the attention of voting members in both houses of the Congress. With time, the public option fell out of favor; the co-ops were examined more closely and considered for the Senate bill.

Senator Kennedy's Death

Edward Kennedy died. A bill was quickly introduced into the Massachusetts Senate allowing the Governor to appoint a temporary replacement. The bill passed 24-16. Governor Deval Patrick appointed Paul G. Kirk, a long time Kennedy aide, to fill the position.

Mayo decided to focus its efforts on health care reform, taking an active rather than a passive role as they had done in the past.

President Obama's job approval slid to 50%. He decided to address both Houses on 9/9/09.

The health care industry chased after "blue dogs" (moderate Democrats), hoping to strengthen its role in Congress.

Senate Markup

The Senate Finance Committee began markup of its bill on 9/22/09, hoping to finish work by the weekend. Three House committees and another Senate committee had produced their versions of health care legislation, written by Democrats and each including a government insurance option to balance private plans. The Senate Finance Committee bill was favored but it quickly realized that its work could not be completed in a week. The "public option" quickly once again proved to be the polarizing factor. It and several other factors (insurance mandate, abortion) slowed progress.

Obama—End the Debate!

August ended and with it the lull in health care news print. On Labor Day, Obama said it was time to end health care debate. His plan for overhauling the nation's health care system was stalled in Congress, largely due to disagreement over the government-run insurance option that would compete with private insurance, but also due to discussion of mandatory insurance, abortion, co-ops, and other matters.

Former Republican Senator Robert Dole said we should start over with a plan that is largely satisfactory to Obama from the beginning.

Obama tried to rescue bipartisan debate with his joint Congressional speech on 9/9/09. He asked Congressmen to stop "bickering" and take action on his plan to overhaul the health care system. One study plan would impose an annual $6 billion tax on health insurers and device manufacturers, e. g., Medtronics, leading the Senate Finance Committee proposal to rely on co-ops rather than on government insurance.

Snow Votes
with the Democrats

Lobbyists fought health care savings efforts. Included were lobbyists for and against the public option, "Cadillac" insurance policies, insurance mandates, and Medicare funds. In the Senate, the Baucus overhaul of health care suffered a blow when Olympia Snow (R-ME) voted with the Democrats to send the bill forward without the public option.

The White House ramped up activity to shape the health bill, e. g., the administration was more hands-on with legislation. The Mayo Clinic and other active interested associations, e. g., the AMA, did the same.

House and Senate Bills

House Speaker Nancy Pelosi of California said, "We are about to deliver on the promise," and then rolled out the House Democrats' bill to extend health care to tens of millions who lack coverage. Senate Majority Leader Harry Reid (D-NV) finalized legislation merging the work of two Senate committees (Finance, Health).

The House bill covered about 96% of residents over 65 years of age and would cost $894 billion over ten years. Democrats said this was under President Obama's $700 billion figure, some of which would come from several sources. The Senate bill seemed to cover 94% and would cost less than $900 billion over ten years. Some of the money would come from insurance companies, drug companies, and medical device manufacturers. Almost everyone would have insurance.

Some observers said the House bill cost too much because the Democrats, deferring to organized labor, refused to draw on the most obvious source of funds, the current tax-free treatment of employer-sponsored health insurance. Others said the debate over the public option was unworthy of so much attention; it would not have that much impact.

HOUSE BILL PASSED

The House bill in fact passed 220-215 on 11/07/09. The upcoming Senate bill would not be voted upon until sometime in January, 2010.

The House of Representatives completed its version of health reform when the Senate was almost ready to begin. Although the House finished deliberations in ten days, the Senate would not be through until the end of the year at least. A lot of procedural and political maneuvering was expected before any amendments could even be debated. The *Christian Science Monitor* explained that at least five areas would be critical to the Senate debate on health care: the public option, cost, payers, coverage, and abortion.

Lobbying to a large extent focused on health insurance and abortion rights, and some of it was unique, e. g., insurers like United Health urged workers to lobby the Senate.

With overhaul in sight, drug prices spiked upward.

Reid was believed to have made several major changes to the bills approved by the Senate Finance and Health Committees in the process of merging them.

George Will said the Democrats' health reform bills were unconstitutional.

A biotech giant (Genontech) waged an aggressive campaign to get its message into the House records of both parties during health reform debates.

The Senate majority leaders' $849 billion plan would require insurance coverage and a government-run plan.

A controversial tax on medical devices, proposed as part of the Senate's landmark health care legislation, was cut in half by Senate negotiators, drawing cautious praise from Medtronic, Inc. and other industry leaders.

Senate Bill Passed

The Democrats posted 60 votes in the Senate showdown, precisely the number needed to overcome Republican delaying tactics. The 60-39 vote on 11/22/09 was a victory for Senate Majority Leader Harry Reid (D-NV) and the White House, and it cleared the way to start debate after the Thanksgiving recess.

The Senate now had to deal with how to expand health coverage to millions of Americans, how to pay for it, whether to include a government-run insurance program, and how to deal with the complex abortion issue. Eight Democratic, Republican, and independent Senators wielded great influence over what and when the Senate decided. These were Harry Reid (D-NV), Ben Nelson (D-NE), Olympia Snow (R-ME), Blanche Lincoln (D-AR), Mitch McConnell (R-KY), Joe Lieberman (I-CT), Roland Burris (D-IL), and Mary Landrieu (D-LA). Their strengths derived from diverse sources.

David Brooks said, "Health care reform won't hit the sweet spot. This boils down to a choice of values: Do we want safety or economic growth?"

Flaring Tempers

Tempers flared during floor debate the day after returning from Thanksgiving recess. One Republican senator said Obama's health care overhaul will shorten the lives of America's seniors by cutting Medicare—shades of the raw charges and countercharges of the summer's town hall meetings.

Reaction from the AMA was hedged. The AMA wrote a letter to the Senate Majority Leader Harry Reid (D-NE) on December 1 concerning the Senate's proposed health system reform bill. The bill represents a melding of previous proposals by the Senate Finance and Health Committees. In the letter, the AMA didn't make a statement of support or opposition to the legislation in its current form. Rather, it said it would reserve judgment until after the Senate floor debate, since there likely would be further changes by then.

On December 3 the Senate voted to approve a women's health measure and turned back a GOP challenge of Medicare costs. Senior congressmen were working out how they would handle many more amendments (there were 92 to deal with). Contentious proposals still awaiting debate were funding for abortion services, tougher requirements on insurance companies, and new rules guiding importation of pharmaceuticals. Rising costs and the Senate schedule were also of concern. The Senate version of the bill would still need to be reconciled with the House version before going to President Obama.

Public Option
and Abortion

Senate moderates held the key to health care fate. Democrats worked to overcome a filibuster, moderates were split on two issues: the public option and abortion. It was hard to see how Reid was going to get 60 votes.

On December 4 the AMA still had not committed itself to a position on the bill.

Medicare

On December 5 the Senate focused its debate on cutting Medicare service. Republicans forced a vote on trimming home care, meant to help pay for the health care bill, but it failed. Four moderate Democrats joined all Republicans in voting for the amendment. Behind closed doors, discussion concerned a solution to the public insurance option. Also of concern were deals cut some time ago which were now in peril. In particular, the hospital, pharmaceutical, and other industries were now being told by fellow Democrats that they were overly generous when their deal was cut earlier in the year.

OBAMA VISITS
SENATE DEMOCRATS

Obama, sensing the hesitancy on Capitol Hill, visited the Senate Democrats on Sunday (December 6) and lobbied Senators to make history on health care. He made no mention of government-run insurance or abortion. After working through the weekend, the Senate was to reconvene Monday to address the abortion issue. An editorial once again warned that the status quo is risky business; reform opponents didn't mention the current system's future costs.

State leaders question whether "opting out" of the public option is a real option or a "sham."

Abortion
Restrictions Blocked

Health care bill's abortion amendment was expected to come to a vote on December 8. Moderate Democrats sought to bar coverage of the procedure if private insurers received federal subsidies. The senate in fact voted on December 8 to block restrictions on abortion funding. If the overall bill cleared the chambers, there would be confrontation with the House over abortion. The vote came on the ninth day of debating the $848 billion, 10 year plan to revamp the nation's health care system.

Ezra Klein of the *Washington Post* pointed out that Americans don't know the true cost of their health care and that employers should show workers the actual health care math.

Broad Agreement?

The Senate majority leader, Harry Reid, said Tuesday night (December 8) that he and a group of 10 Democratic senators had reached a "broad agreement" to resolve a dispute over the government-run health insurance plan that has posed the biggest obstacle to passage of sweeping health care legislation. Reid refused to provide details and others said there was no deal. The proposal was sent to the CBO for analysis.

It appeared that the overhaul bill would be phased in slowly (over the next three to four years) and that the Senate was considering expanding Medicare to people as young as 55 years old. The Mayo Clinic Health Policy Center said this would reduce access, compromise quality, and increase costs.

CBO Estimate

The CBO estimated the cost of the Senate plan. A family of four earning $54,000 in 2016, when the plan would be in effect, would be eligible for a subsidy of $10,000. Monthly premiums would cost $825. Some people ages 55 to 64 could "buy in" starting in 2011. That would cost $7600 a year per person or $15,200 for a couple. No subsidies would be available until 2014. The Medicare option would be available only to the uninsured. The figures generated the term "sticker shock."

There was more sobering news on Friday (December 12) from the Health and Humane Services Department. It found that the nation's $2.5 trillion annual health care tab won't shrink under the plan that senators are debating. Instead, it would grow more rapidly than if Congress does nothing.

More troubling was the report's assessment that the plan would decrease services if $493 billion over 10 years were squeezed from Medicare. The report also warned that a new long-term-care insurance plan risks failure because it would attract people in poor health, leading to higher premiums.

December 13 brought more complaints about the plan to enroll aging baby boomers in Medicare. The program would be far from free and would make it harder for seniors to get medical care. This generated a letter of complaint from 10 senators to Senate Majority Leader Harry Reid.

On Monday December 14, Democrats scrambled to get health care votes. The next 48 hours was seen to be critical to the fate of reform in the Senate, as Democratic leaders struggled to settle disputes that stood in the way of holding a final vote this year on the massive package ($848 billion). Most of the undecided lawmakers refused to commit until CBO delivered a cost analysis on the coverage alternatives offered in the preceding week. This was the alternative to the government insurance option. Other stumbling blocks included importation of drugs from foreign countries and abortion coverage.

Small business owners were particularly critical of reform, especially the House version. Employers feared bigger insurance bills and government penalties if they didn't play along. They thought pending bills had too many mandates and too little cost control. For small businesses, costs would go up, not down, cost being the main problem with the current system.

Medicare Abandoned

On December 16, the Senate moved to abandon the Medicare expansion plan. Senate Democratic leaders, scrambling for 60 votes for the health care overhaul, had moved Monday (December 14) to strike the proposal for expanding Medicare and also proceed without a new government insurance program. Senator Tom Harkin (D-IA) said, "There's enough good in this bill even without those two; we've got to move it." Senator Joe Lieberman was encouraged by the direction the discussion was going.

Obama Meets with Senate Democrats

President Obama met with the entire Senate Democratic caucus, prodding Senators to "Seize the Moment." Despite deep divisions, he appealed to Democrats' sense of history, and urged them to act on health care. Afterward he declared himself "cautiously optimistic." The meeting underscored the sense of urgency for Obama. Senator Reid said he would move to terminate debate on Friday (December 18) and vote on December 23 or 24. The House had approved its version of the bill some time ago. Senator Joe Lieberman (I-CT) was at center stage with his threats to block the bill. Some progress was made on Tuesday (December 15); the Senate rejected a bipartisan proposal to allow importation of prescription drugs from other countries. It also turned down a GOP effort to revise a bill to eliminate any tax increase on individuals with incomes less than $200,000 a year. Abortion was still under discussion.

Focus Shifted to Nelson

On December16, the "power of one" shifted from Lieberman to Ben Nelson, Democrat from Nebraska, as the lone holdout. The effort to win his support hinged largely on abortion policy, the same issue that nearly derailed action on the health care bill at the last minute in the House. Nelson met with president Obama three times in the last nine days. This and a variety of GOP delaying tactics brought debate to a halt for a time. To support Nelson, a wide array of Democrats reached out to him, including former senators Tom Daschle of South Dakota and Bob Kerry of Nebraska.

Efforts to win Nelson's vote continued on December 17, as the Senate raced against the clock. Reid planned 'round the clock' sessions during the following week, hoping to find that critical 60th vote by Christmas.

An ABC News/W Post poll showed that 53% disapproved of how Obama was handling health care, and a majority opposed the Senate bill.

Judd Gregy, U. S. Senator from New Hampshire, summarized the Republican point of view when he said, "We need health care reform, but this isn't the right bill—we in Congress have the responsibility to produce meaningful health reform, but we must do so in the right way so as not to create another brand-new big government entitlement program that will cause further damage to our already crumbling basal structure."

The Senate continued to focus on Nelson on December 18, hoping to lock down the 60 votes necessary. His main concern was abortion funding, but he had a number of other needs that would require more funds.

Senator Nelson
Switched His Vote

On December 19 (Saturday), Senator Ben Nelson (D-NE) announced that he would vote for health care reform when it came up for a cloture vote in the Senate, early in the following week. Senate Majority Leader Harry Reid revealed the final package of changes to the bill, known as the manager's amendment, on Saturday morning. They reflected Nelson's demands regarding abortion and Medicare reimbursement rate in Nebraska specifically. Nelson warned that his ultimate vote would not be assured until he saw the results of the Conference Committee. There was some question whether a formal conference would in fact be held. Much of the deliberation was behind closed doors.

TROUBLES LAY AHEAD

Obama said he got 95% of his priorities (see Krauthammer above for another view), but troubles lay ahead, particularly concerning the public option, abortion, and uneven health coverage for some states. The White House urged marathon talks. On the other hand, it appeared that this years' health reform would be just the first step in a long process. The Senate plan had the edge, but the difficult question was how to pay for the reforms. To complicate matters, the American Association of Medical Colleges (AAMC) said the USA would have a shortfall in physicians of 125,000 by 15 years, a serious problem considering how long it takes to produce a physician. George Will again said health care legislation, as proposed, was illegal. Obama's approval rating dropped to 46%. Krauthammer said Obama was paying the priced for misreading his mandate. The Massachusetts race to select a replacement for Edward Kennedy could place the health reform bill in peril. If the Republicans won there, the entire health care bill could be threatened.

The liberal Democrats were finding it difficult to vote for a bill without a public option and with new restrictions on abortion funding. Another sticky point was the Senate proposal that high cost "Cadillac" health plans be subject to a new excise tax.

Senator Scott Brown

Meanwhile, campaigns were progressing in Massachusetts for the Senate seat vacated by Edward Kennedy. Surprisingly, polls suggested that the Republican candidate, Scott Brown, would win the seat. This was in fact what happened on January 19, 2010, changing the composition of the US Senate and placing the health care reform bill in jeopardy. Krauthammer said the GOP win in Massachusetts was in fact all about health care reform.

Options Few and Uncertain

Options were now few and uncertain. The most obvious path would be to pass the bill that cleared the Senate on Christmas Eve. House leaders could pass the Senate bill and then try to fix it using the fast track budget procedure known as "reconciliation." Or the Democrats could scrap the health care measures and then start over in the Senate to a drastically scaled back reconciliation bill. Or the Democrats could simply shelve their grand vision to expand coverage to millions of people who cannot afford it and revert to a bare bones measure that would include some of the more popular initiatives in the existing bills.

Give Up? Obama Says No and Invites GOP to Another Summit

After much discussion, Pelosi said they decided they could not pass the Senate health care bill in the House and the White House bowed to the need to pass on health care. Health care was dropped from the grand scheme.

However, in his State of the Union Address, Obama urged lawmakers not to abandon the health care reform bill, although he didn't offer guidance on how Congress should reconcile the differences between the House and the Senate versions of the bill. And the Mayo Clinic said, "Health reform must succeed!" Katherine Kersten asked whether bipartisan health care is possible. She concluded that it is, but suggested it should have three goals—lower costs, increased access, and greater citizen control over health care (the most effective reforms won't cost anything, e. g., allow people to buy insurance across state lines). The *Minneapolis Star Tribune* said it's time to reframe health care reform and make strengthened protection of consumers a priority, premiums affordable, shore up Medicare, and give states flexibility.

U. S. Representative Michelle Bachmann said, "We aren't going to give up. We're not going to quit fighting because a government takeover of health care is the 'Crown Jewel of Socialism.'"

Obama invited the GOP to a summit. Krauthammer said that Obama and parties like his interpret the Massachusetts election results to mean that the voters are dumb!

"Plan B"

The House breaks out plan B for health care reform—removing the antitrust exemption enjoyed by the health insurance companies and then pealing off some popular items and trying to pass them.

Obama's "new" plan.

1. Require individuals to buy insurance.
2. Expand subsidies to help families afford coverage.
3. Close Medicare "doughnut hole."
4. Allow federal oversight on insurance rate.
5. Impose new tax on unearned income of the wealthy.

Some said the new plan was really not different from the previous plan. Results of the Summit on March 25—no progress!

Summit Results

The Democrats had to go it alone. The question of using reconciliation was repeatedly addressed. The challenge for Obama was now getting a bill approved by the end of next month. The Summit was a remarkably sustained, detailed, and deeply felt debate, but the same fundamental differences remained. Seven and a half hours of debate only widened the gulf. Unbending Republican Opposition!

David Lightman said the potential for a bipartisan breakthrough existed, but the obstacles were plenty. The desperate Democrats may grasp the shortest route (reconciliation—"nuclear option") with the risk of poisoning the water.

Pelosi Said Follow Obama

Pelosi said the House was to follow Obama's health blueprint. She said the president's solution to stay firm could help Democrats wrap up debate on overhaul before March 26. Two voting blocs were pivotal to the health overhaul future: abortion opponents and fiscal conservatives.

On March 1, 2010, White House adviser Nancy-Ann DeParle said she thought Democrats would secure enough votes on the measure, and signaled that the administration could be moving toward trying to pass it along party lines. Increasingly, the White House appeared to favor having the House pass a version of the measure that cleared the Senate with 60 votes in December. The Senate would then pass changes to the bill to ratify some demands of House Democrats. The Senate vote would take place under the parliamentary procedure known as reconciliation, which required 51 votes rather than 60. It was unclear whether the Democrats had enough votes within their ranks for this strategy to work.

Pelosi Optimistic

On March 1 Pelosi also expressed confidence in the health care vote, saying that she would have enough votes to pass a health care overhaul, but acknowledged that it could come at a political cost to lawmakers who back the measure.

Obama Points the Way

March 3. Obama points the way forward. In preparing for a speech on Wednesday March 3, he rejected the Republicans preferred approach of scrapping the existing bills and starting over. Instead, he said he was open to four Republican ideas, namely 1) containing abuse and fraud, particularly in Medicare and Medicaid, 2) specialized health courts for malpractice, 3) health savings accounts, and 4) increased reimbursements to Medicaid providers.

The Final Push

Obama's final push! In the strongest language yet, on March 3, the President sought to fast-track the health care overhaul, urging Democrats to pass it within weeks, saying "The American people are waiting for us to act," even if it requires the Democrats to go forward without the Republicans, using reconciliation. This would cover 31 million uninsured Americans, require Americans to get insurance, require insurers to accept all clients, require drug makers to help seniors afford medicine, reduce the budget deficit by about one trillion dollars over the next two decades, and cost about 100 billion dollars per year.

CBO APPROVAL

On March 7, Peter Orzag and Nancy Ann DeParle (Director of the Office of Management and Budget and Director of the White House Office of Health Reform, respectively) argued that the critics were wrong, that the President's Health Plan is not fiscally flawed, but to the contrary, it is fiscally responsible and doable. For example, skeptics have claimed that the $100 billion in deficit reduction the President's plan would achieve over the next decade is mere gimmickry. Orzag and DeParle explained why this is not the case.

Columnist Ed Dionne said reconciliation would be used to "ram through" the entire health bill. It would apply to amendments dealing with money issues. That's what it's for!

Final Push on the Road

Obama, feeling that his signature legislative initiative was far from certain, decided to take a last ditch push on the road. In a speech in Philadelphia, he tried to persuade the public and congressmen that his plan is worthy of support despite inherent dangers at the polls. He struck a populist tone, setting up the health insurance industry as his main target. "We can't have a system that works better for insurance companies than it does for the American people," he said.

Representative Stupak (D-MI) and Abortion

Another stumbling block for House passage was the renewed objection of Representative Bart Stupak for federal funding of abortions. Debate got to the point where a small bloc of antiabortion Democrats held the key to final passage of health insurance reform legislation. And what does the Stupak-Obama compromise, memorialized in an executive order, mean? Clarification would undoubtedly follow.

POLITICAL COURAGE

Editorials were soon calling for political courage--the status quo is more frightening than political maneuvering. As one of the few people who fully understood the reconciliation process, parliamentarian Alan Frumin was called upon for guidance. The Democrats garnered encouragement from commitments of support from liberals in the House, where defections were most feared, e. g., abortion opponents. Undecided Democrats also wanted assurance on cost. The Democratic leaders were still nowhere near the 216 votes they needed to pass the health care bill in the House. House Speaker Pelosi said she might forgo a showdown vote on the Senate-passed bill and have a House vote only on a separate package of unpalatable amendments, e. g., the "cornhuskers' kickback" and the "slaughters' solution." On March 17, Democrats were searching in Congress for shortcut approval. Critics were alarmed and questioned the plans constitutionally.

MORE HEAT FROM OBAMA

Obama turned up the Heat on House Democrats even more. There was some movement. Representative Oberstar, an abortion opponent, said he would not stand in the way of a final bill. Others credited large insurance rate hikes, e. g., 39% in California, with reviving health care reform.

CBO ANALYSIS

Finally, the Democrats revealed a $940 billion bill, but they were buoyed by a CBO analysis showing cuts in the deficit. They therefore began a countdown to a Sunday vote in 10 days.

On March 20, Democrats narrowed the hunt to a dozen positive votes. Obama prepared to meet with Democrats at a final rally on Saturday.

Scrutiny of the CBO figures showed that the Obama plan only slows the premium rise; it does not eliminate it. Discussion was widespread. Obama said that momentum was building.

It's in Your Hands

Obama continued to ramp up the drive for health care reform. He told Congress, "It's in your hands. Do it for the American people." Thousands rallied in Washington on the Mall. The Tea Party tried to refocus politics. (It was a grass roots movement whose number and influence remained a mystery. It was credited with helping elect Massachusetts Senator Scott Brown.)

On March 19, pushing toward a Sunday vote that could transform the national health insurance system, House leaders announced a $940 billion compromise on Thursday that would

1. Extend coverage to most Americans.
2. Cut billions of dollars from Medicare.
3. Impose new taxes on the wealthy and the well insured.

The Democrats were buoyed by the new cost analysis showing an apparent reduction in the deficit.

PASSED!

The House passed the health bill on Sunday, March 21, 2010, after a final day of drama searching for a dozen yea votes, Democrats were still making adjustments to the bill the next day ("reconciliation bill"). There was not a single Republican yea vote. The Republicans were furious and objected vigorously. Dozens of them signed a pledge for the Fall election: "We will repeal it." The Tea Party said it was not going to stop. The overhaul was a rallying cry that made the party more focused than ever. Republican attorneys general in 14 states sued together or separately to overturn the law, arguing that Congress exceeded its authority in passing it.

Congressional Democrats helped deliver Obama's health care overhaul. Now dozens of them were politically impaired with a November election approaching. Can he save their seats?

Some said the Medicare cuts don't add up. "We can't ring the register twice." President Obama signed the bill on Tuesday, saying "We mark a new season in America."

Final Chapter?

Is this the final chapter? The Tea Party activists and Republicans said they were not going to stop. The passage of health care simply refocused their activity. After a full year of vigorous effort, it is clear that there is no easy way to pay for comprehensive health care reform. Realistically, funding will probably have to come from a combination of sources, some of them not yet fiscally visited. If combinations yield less revenue than needed, Obama may have to retreat from his goal of providing all Americans with comprehensive insurance. Partial solutions such as limiting benefits or phasing in any expansion of coverage are possible.

Some reactions were predictable. On April 9 Stupak bowed out. The embattled leader of the Democrats' anti-abortion forces during the health care debate announced that he would not seek re-election.

Health insurers jockeyed for advantage; firms reshaped policies with one eye on the new law and the other eye on the bottom line. Some said that these insurers would try to cherry-pick as much as they could get away with between November and when the legislation is fully implemented.

The Stupak-Pitts antiabortion amendment deserves special attention. The amendment was co-authored by

Congressman Joe Pitts (R-PA) and Bart Stupak (D-MI). Pitts focused on the last minute deal between Stupak and the White House, in which Stupak (and a half-dozen colleagues) would vote for the final bill without amendments if the President agreed to sign an executive order ensuring enforcement of the Hyde amendment explicitly applying to the federal funding provided under health care reform, a long standing prohibition against the use of federal funds for abortion. President Obama signed the executive order restricting abortion funding on March 24, at a private White House event. The order aimed to establish adequate enforcement mechanisms to ensure that federal funds were not used for abortion services (except in the case of rape or when the life of the mother is endangered) consistent with the long standing Federal resolution that is commonly known as the Hyde amendment. These agreements may have influenced the last minute voting on the health bill.

Equally important is the problem of shortage of primary care physicians. Newly insured citizens may not be able to find a doctor. R. A. Cooper said that amidst intense discussions about health care reform, too little attention has been paid to the fact that the United States is entering an era of physician shortages. Never before have shortages of the magnitude now developing existed, nor was the United States ever so far behind in responding. Most remarkably, although shortages in nearly every field of medicine are recognized by political leaders, health care planning is proceeding as though no severe problems exist.

The health care bill was politics (as usual). Obama may eventually claim victory, but he didn't change how it was done. Bipartisanship is as distant as ever.

ABOUT THE AUTHOR

He was born and raised in Minnesota and had all his schooling in Minnesota, including training in internal medicine at the Mayo Clinic and a PhD in physiology from the University of Minnesota. His entire career was spent in teaching and research, and he was a chairman of physiology for most of the period. He lived in several states, most recently in Washington, DC, and during that time was a consultant to NASA life sciences research. He has been married to his pediatrician wife for 64 years, and they have three children and seven grandchildren. He and his wife moved to Rochester, Minnesota, ten years ago. His special interests include painting acrylic landscapes, golfing, and attending Mayo Clinic seminars. He also reviews papers for several medical journals.

www.ingramcontent.com/pod-product-compliance
Lightning Source LLC
Chambersburg PA
CBHW020356290526
45785CB00005B/2313